Necco® Sweethearts®

I LOVE WORDS

Barbara Barbieri McGrath

Charlesbridge

LOVE TO: Kathleen Morse.

KISSES TO: Donna Armstrong and the staff at
Ezra Baker Elementary School in Dennis, Massachusetts.

HUGS TO: Lois MacGregor, Reading Specialist,
Hastings Elementary School in Westboro, Massachusetts.

Text copyright © 2003 by Barbara Barbieri McGrath
Illustrations copyright © 2003 by Charlesbridge Publishing

Published by Charlesbridge
85 Main Street
Watertown, MA 02472
(617) 926-0329
www.charlesbridge.com

Library of Congress Cataloging-in-Publication Data

McGrath, Barbara Barbieri, 1954–
 I love words / Barbara Barbieri McGrath.
    p. cm.
Summary: Introduces the letters of the alphabet and simple words,
including colors, numbers, compound words, and contractions, using Necco®
Sweethearts® candies.
 ISBN 1-57091-567-9 (reinforced for library use) — ISBN 1-57091-568-7 (softcover)
 1. Lexicology—Juvenile literature. [1. Vocabulary. 2. Alphabet. 3.
Reading readiness.] I. Title.
 P326 .M38 2003
 428.1—dc21   2002155448

Printed in South Korea

(hc) 10 9 8 7 6 5 4 3 2 1
(sc) 10 9 8 7 6 5 4 3 2 1

Display type set in Hoosker Do, designed by T-26 of Chicago, IL, USA, Segura Inc.'s Digital Type Foundry,
     started by Carlos Segura in 1994; text type set in Adobe Caslon
Printed and bound by Pacifica Comunications, South Korea
Production supervision by Brian G. Walker
Designed by Susan Mallory Sherman

Let's learn to read words. There's no time like now.
You'll love to read once you know how.

Here are the letters *A* through Z.
Uppercase and lowercase letters to see.

Each letter has its own special sound.
To begin to make words, move them around.

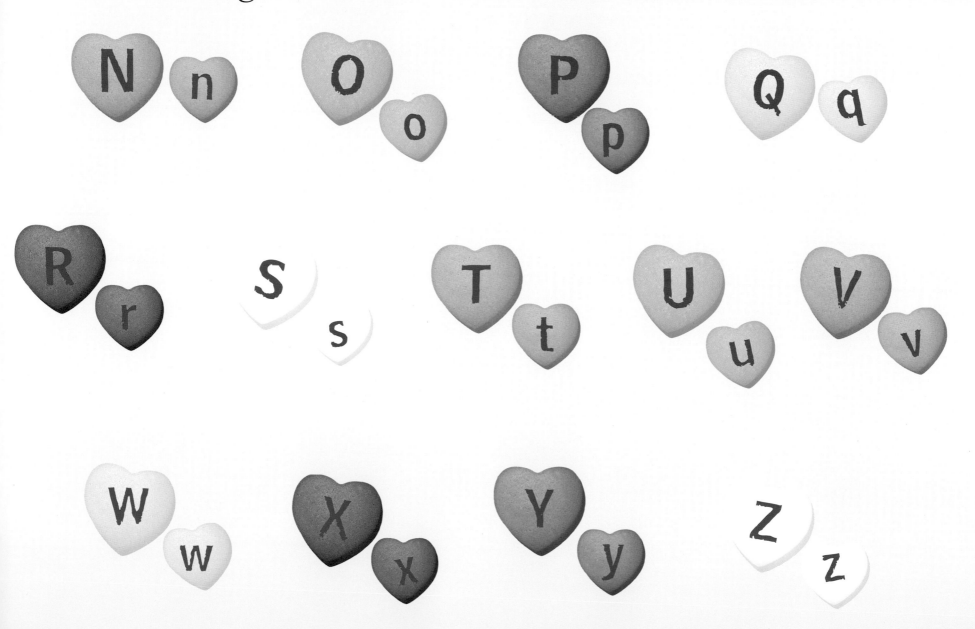

Use vowels so that the words are heard.
They're an important part of every word.

Pat, pet, pit, pot, put, oh my...
A vowel can sometimes be a *Y*.

A long vowel "a" means you hear *A* in **say.**

The short "a" in **can** does not sound that way.

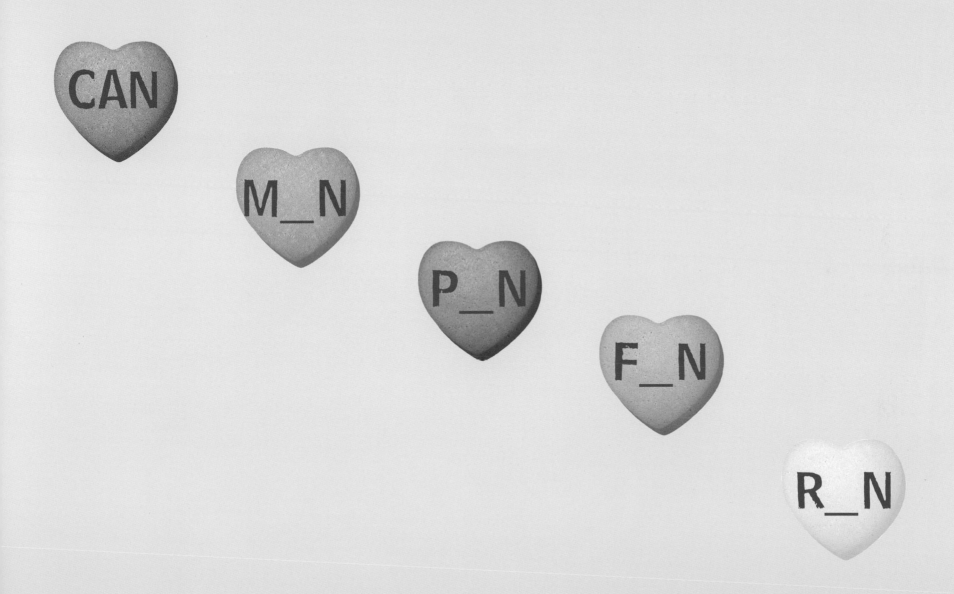

Try words without vowels. No matter how hard you try...

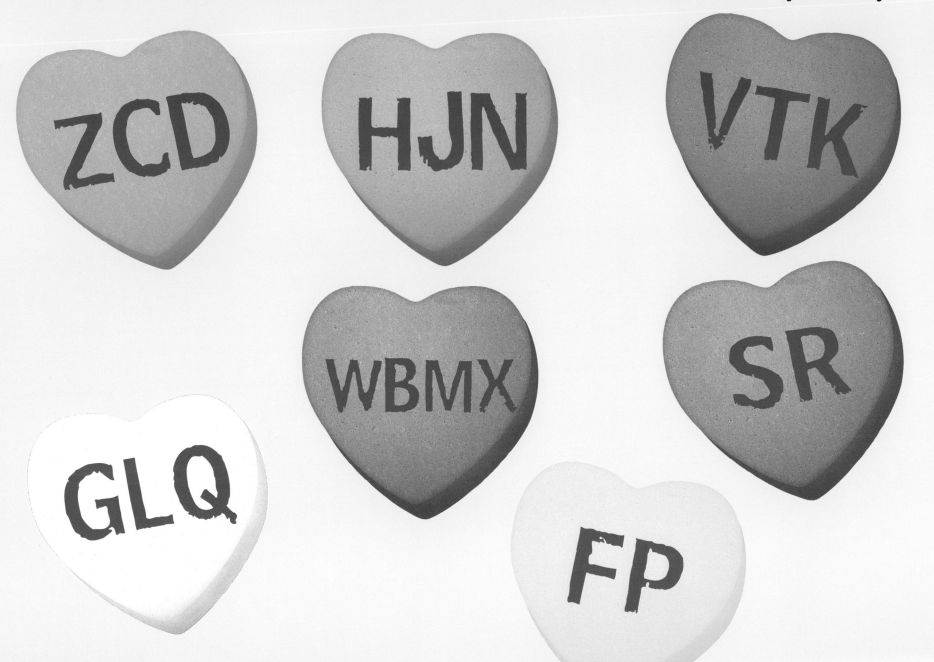

Consonants need vowels. And now you know why.

Look at these words with all your might;
Try to know them all by sight.

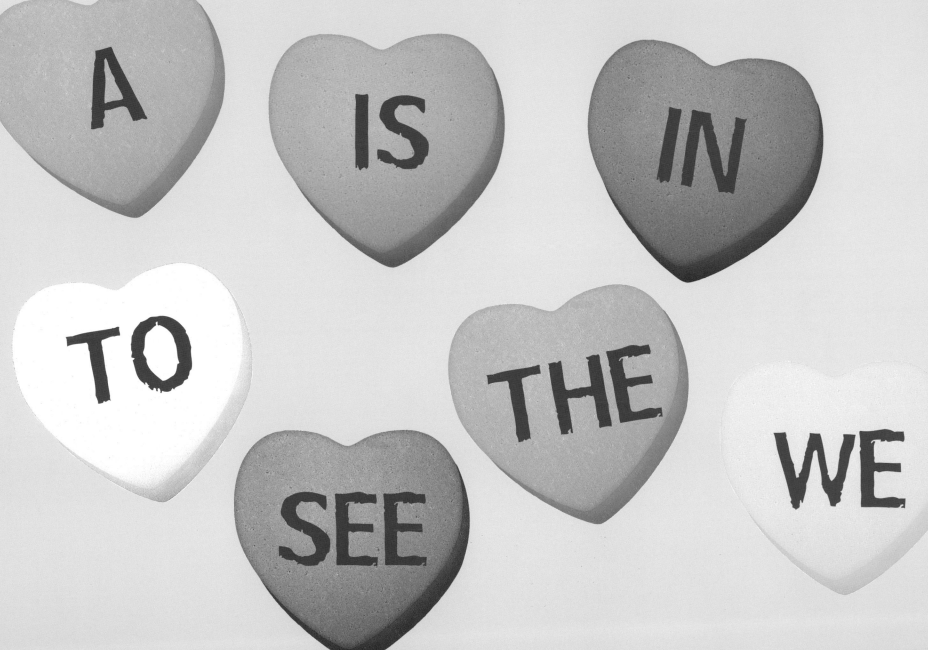

A, is, in, to, see, the, we.
And, I, can, up, go, it, me.

While reading words you will learn to spell—
Met, made, bus, home, this, box, tell.

MET

MADE

BUS

HOME

BOX

TELL

THIS

That was fun. Let's try some more—
Day, out, food, think, time, said, for!

Run, red, cat, big, come, like, look.
Here, play, this, on, read a book!

Look closely to read: **the, they, there, that, then.**
Words can answer—**Who? What? Where? Why? When?**

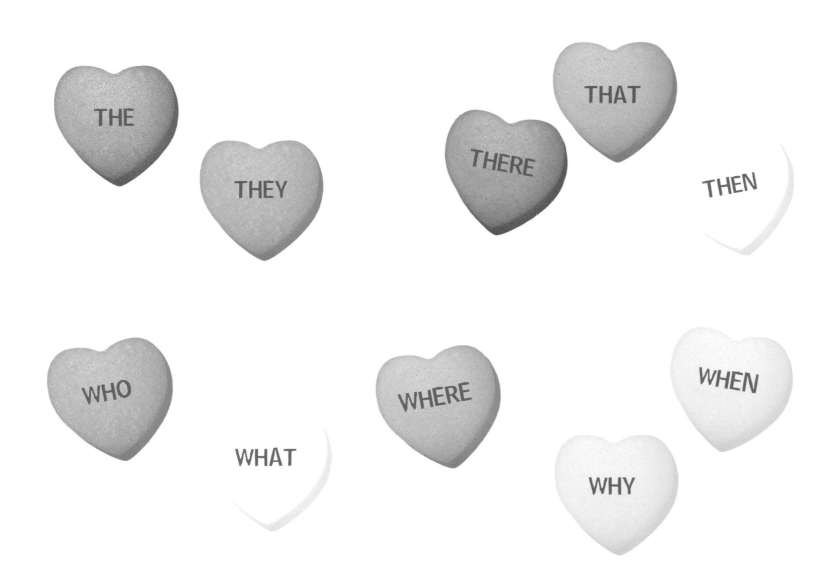

These words are the numbers from **one** to **ten**.
To know them well, read them again.

Purple, orange, green, yellow, pink, and white.
The words mean the color. Did you read them right?

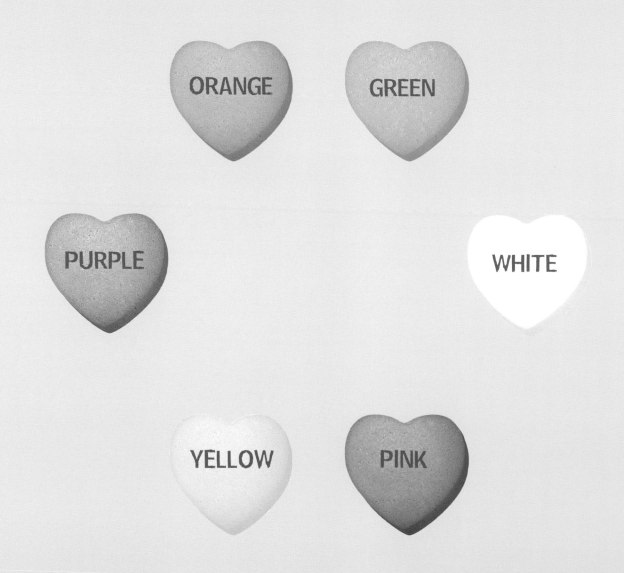

Here are more colors for you to do.
Read each one: **red, black, brown, blue.**

RED   BLACK   BROWN   BLUE

Contractions are two words turned into one.
An apostrophe means the job's been done.
Has not is **hasn't, will not** is **won't.**
Is not is **isn't, do not** is **don't.**

HAS + NOT = HASN'T

WILL + NOT = WON'T

IS + NOT = ISN'T

DO + NOT = DON'T

Compound words can be a lot of fun.
Find two words that make up one.

Upstairs, sometime, and **rainbow**,
Bedtime, sunshine. Now you know.

Words that sound alike are said to rhyme.
You can learn to do it in no time.
Make–cake, book–look, see–me–tree.
Jump–bump, big–pig, he–knee–three.

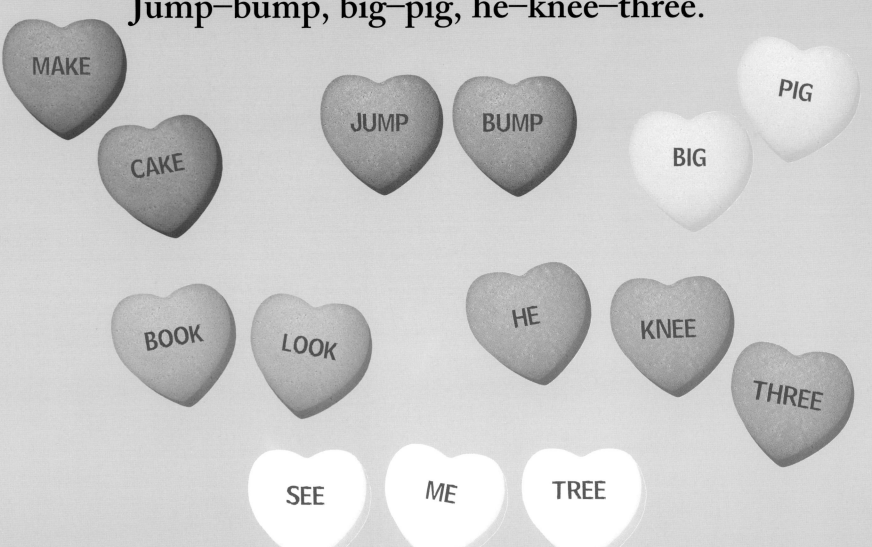

Hop–pop, box–fox, go–no–grow.
Feet–meet, ring–sing, low–tow–show.

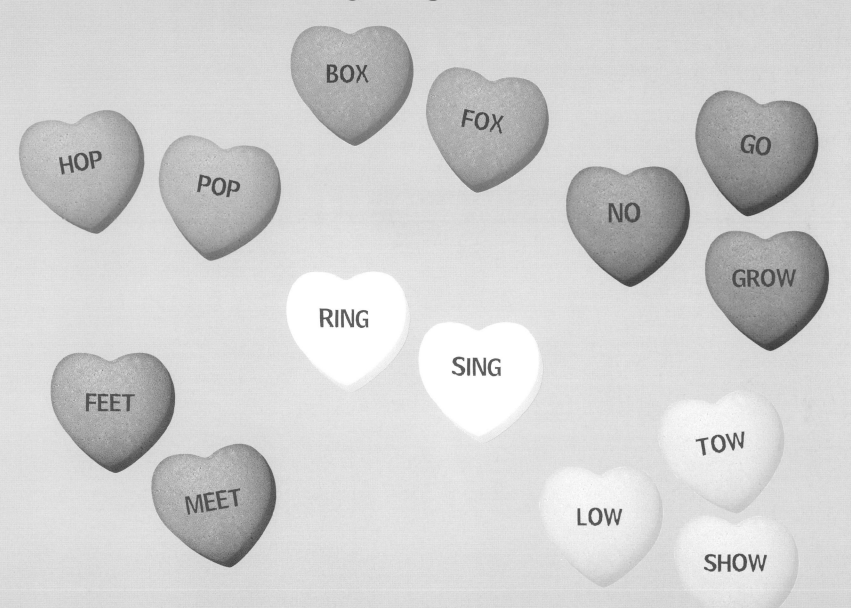

Opposite words are far from the same.
Think of some—it's like a game!
On–**off**, **up**–**down**, **stop** and **go**.
Push–**pull**, **in**–**out**, **yes** and **no**.

ON

OFF

PUSH

UP

PULL

DOWN

STOP

IN

YES

GO

OUT

NO

These opposite words might make you grin.
Big–small, short–tall, fat and **thin**.

Dog, cat, bird, sheep, bear, and **snake.**
Words say the sounds that these words make.

Woof, meow, tweet, baa, roar, and hiss.
Did you know reading would sound like this?

Words make you feel good for a long while.
Hello, **hug**, **kiss**, **good**, **love**, and **smile**.

Call me. Be mine. You're my friend ...

I LOVE WORDS

THIS IS

THE END